TO BEN & RUBY

THE FEEL-GOOD ALPHABET BOOK

WRITTEN BY LISA CALHOUN OWEN
ILLUSTRATED BY JORDAN WRAY

Dream BIG!
Lisa C. Owen
2021

Copyright © 2021 by Lisa Calhoun-Owen. All rights reserved. This book may not be reproduced or stored in whole or in part by any means without the written permission of the author except for brief quotations for the purpose of review.

Editor: Amy Ashby

ISBN: 978-1-954614-21-5 Hard Cover
ISBN: 978-1-954614-22-2 Soft Cover

Published by Warren Publishing
Charlotte, NC
www.warrenpublishing.net
Printed in the United States

In memory of
Bonnie McBride Calhoun and Carroll Ray Calhoun
The end of an era.

and

Dedicated to
Jayden Scott Reilly and Everley Rose Davenport
The new beginning.

If I were an **A**,

I'd be ≡AWESOME≡ I know,

ALWAYS up for Adventures

ready... set... **GO!**

IF I WERE an **E**,

I'd BE **EAGER** TO LEARN,

PAY attention IN SCHOOL,

AND wait FOR MY TURN.

If I were a **G**,

I'd be the color of **GOLD**

and shine like the sun,

so **BRIGHT** and so **BOLD**.

If I were an **H,**
I'd be **HONEST** as can be,
treating others with RESPECT
just like I want them to treat ME.

IF I WERE a K, I'd ALWAYS BE KIND, I'd be HONEST and HELPFUL ALL of the time.

If I were an L,
I'd LOVE everyone,
treat them all the same,
and have lots of FUN!

IF I WERE an **M**, I'd simply BE **MAGNIFICENT**, CELEBRATING who we are, AND the Things that make us DIFFERENT.

IF I WERE an **N, NOW** I'D START right to be a good person and make everyone proud.

If I were an O, I'd OPEN my eyes WIDE to see the WORLD around me, from the OCEANS to the SKY.

IF I WERE a **P**,
I'D BE SWEET AS **PIE**,
I'D ALWAYS tell the **TRUTH**
and NEVER, EVER **LIE**.

If I were an **R**, I'd RUN, RUN all day! I'd enjoy lots of SUNSHINE, EXERCISE, and PLAY.

If I were an  S,
I'd SMILE and GRIN,
and FEEL those GOOD feelings
SHINE from within.

If I were a **T**, I'd work **TOGETHER** to do ALL I can and make the WORLD BETTER.

IF I WERE a U, YOU would be my BEST FRIEND! WE WOULD LAUGH and PLAY until the daylight ENDS.

IF I WERE a  **VALIANT**,

I'D BE FEARLESS and

I'D FACE MY GREATEST FEAR,

BE BRAVE, and challenge it.

IF I WERE A **W**, I'd know I am **WORTH** MORE than money or ANYthing on this whole wide EARTH.

If I were an X, I'd be an eX-cellent KID and HELP other children wherever they live.

If I were a Y, I'd say YUMMY, YUMMY, and eat GOOD things for my HUNGRY little tummy.

IF I WERE a **Z**, I'd try my BEST to be **ZAPPY**, which is a SUPER FUN way to say, "ALWAYS BE HAPPY!"

CPSIA information can be obtained
at www.ICGtesting.com
Printed in the USA
BVHW021947230521
606837BV00001B/2